In the Drift of Words

Selected works of William Oxley

Poetry:

The Notebook of Hephaestus and Other Poems
(Lomond Press, 1981)
A Map of Time (University of Salzburg, 1984)
The Mansands' Trilogy (Keepsake Press, 1988)
Mad Tom on Tower Hill (Stride, 1988)
Forest Sequence (Mammon Press, 1991)
The Patient Reconstruction of Paradise
(Acumen Publications, 1991)
Forthcoming:
Cardboard Troy and Other Poems (Stride, 1993)

Translations:

Poems of a Black Orpheus (L.S. Senghor)
(The Menard Press, 1981)
Forthcoming:
Ghazals & Other Poems of Hafiz (trans. with Parvin Loloi)

Prose:

Of Human Consciousness (University of Salzburg, 1982)
The Idea & Its Imminence (University of Salzburg, 1982)
The Cauldron of Inspiration (University of Salzburg, 1983)
The Inner Tapestry (University of Salzburg, 1985)
Of Poets and Poetry: Letters between a Father and Son.
Edited by Patricia Oxley (University of Salzburg, 1988)
Distinguishing Poetry.   Edited by Glyn Pursglove
(University of Salzburg, 1989)

William Oxley

In the Drift
of Words

Rockingham Press
1992

Published in 1992
by
The Rockingham Press
11 Musley Lane,
Ware, Herts
SG12 7EN

British Library Cataloguing-in-Publication Data

A catalogue record for this book
is available from the British Library

ISBN 1 873468 09 1

Printed in Great Britain
by Biddles Limited,
Guildford

Printed on Recycled Paper

Supported by the **Eastern Arts** Board

To Patricia, Glyn and Acumen

'Annihilating all that's made
To a green thought in a green shade'

Andrew Marvell
The Garden

Acknowledgements

Some of the poems in this collection first appeared in *Acumen, Ambit, The Arcadian, Encounter, Envoi, The Green Book, Interactions, New Welsh Review, The Observer, Odyssey, Other Poetry, Outposts, The Pen, Pennine Platform, Poetry & Audience, The Scotsman, The Spectator, Spokes, Tracks* and *Westwords.* 'A Critic in Brighton' was published in *Derek Stanford, Man of Letters: A Tribute at 70* (Acumen Publications); 'Some Irregularics for Barbara Hepworth' appeared in *Hepworth: A Celebration,* published by Westwords; and 'Growing Acorns in Islington' was published as a broadsheet by Turret Books. The quotation from P. J. Kavanagh which introduces 'An Admonition' is from his poem 'Yeats' Tower' which appeared in his collection *Presences* (Chatto & Windus, 1987). Thanks are due to all the editors and publishers involved.

Contents

In the Drift of Words

City of shadows and cries
Through which so many days slide,
Have slid on the thin film of memory.
Appalling death so much you hide!
Old friends gone like vanished
Games of cricket, their talks, loves
Now nothing but words and poignant
Sepia of so many faded photographs.

City of shadows and cries
Built of ambition and such neglect.
Love-that-might-have-been
Walks the dry circuitry of an ever-new
Ever more technological round;
And the church by the hedge, the
Birds under echoing elms,
The brazen joy of brook and field:

Scenery, a backdrop only for motorways.
One hope now lives, it does,
And that dwells among words.
Stop, look, listen you fools,
Stars shed their light on night words
And in the day are summer words still
Which yet will curb the turbulent heart
And move it to stand beating
On the summit of some grass-blown green hill.

Art and Mammon

The City, that accountants' joy, made him
Made me. Within its great grey O throng
Tortured players and makers of song
Merchants and madmen, men out to win
The racing rat ride from virtue to sin.
Hell of Bankside, hurrying river, Paul's,
The holy bars of brokerage and booze;
Men aftershaved and girls cosmetic-smooth
Purposely striding glass and marble halls.
Here Tom o'Bedlam, me and that better Will
We found a fearsome matrix for our skill.
And words were henceforth haunted by it still;
That City whose sweet sessions of memory
Are blessed by a bitter paradox: money.

A Triolet on the Social Life

Phoning people fixing dates
     Do you really wish to know 'em?
It's all a game of love and hates
     Phoning people fixing dates:
The duty of it often grates
     Like the metre of this poem.
Phoning people fixing dates —
     Do you really wish to know 'em?

No Annus Mirabilis

How wrong Larkin was
about everything save loss
(and that, too, is only a guess?)
for the barriers never came down.
Only one thing is surely known
as certain as sin's wages
or youth's unhappy urges:
nothing ever really changes.

Is there Life after Concrete?

Cars like greasy prunes
roll smoothly down
to the intestinal city
and return in the bilious evening.
This is commerce, nothing else.

Here days and nights are
electrostatic
time and the stars crackle
in black shook nylon.
Over the horizon men make war.

Watch the intricate dance
of green leaves
outside intent glass
how still their framed immediacy!
Is there life after concrete,
or do we settle
for the tender caress of memory
leaves desiring windows?

Walking among Friends is a Thousand Memories

'A curse on me that I did not write with joy'
DOUGLAS DUNN

Walking among friends is a thousand memories
of places, holy places of feeling;
I choose to walk in the sunlight's shade,
the cars coughing and barking at me like slave dogs
and still I write with joy of joy because
we can all summon-up the love that is no loss
even in reality's dirty places, its fear-lined
battered woman-face and its scientific facts.

The world is a stinking dustbin of light, the
very finest things made the butt of an incredible joke,
intellectuals the sour foreskins of modern despair,
and in laboratories of the aborted heart everything will be cloned
save unpredictable happiness because
no cancer they say has ever died of love.

Yet I can praise on Rosslyn Hill or Finchley Road
the wine-dark days of life, having seen through the black hole
of all my deaths and seen this: a vast summoning
in the minds of everyone who has ever lived in which
each memory dies into an intimate, changeless present.

Walking among friends is a thousand memories
called up like them, their angel selves, and
however strong time's steel between the suffering
and pain (expunged only by brief moments of love)
walking among friends is sharing loveliest joy
that untouchable flower beneath an ocean of glass.

Growing Acorns in Islington

Smashing, the effect of the brown
leaf-storm like great coils and curls
of rusty barbed-wire blown
down along luminous lawns,
slopes of London-nature that belong
to tired metropolites,
towards the shimmering plonk
of underhill ponds
where Highgate greenly dreams.

A moment after, the sepia-
and-gold bluster of autumn passed,
we found the acorn shower lying still.
And now I hear two tiny spheres
of that day's life are at rooting rest,
potted in 'gentle Charles's' grimy
Islington where skies are
cemetery-grey but forever fertile.

We live through others' eyes
more than our own, and
over pigeon-slated roofs I gaze
and think where poet Leonard lies
in Islington — who loved the earth of Heath
and Highgate too — and my mind flies
into newer lives again
where one would nurture bonsai oak
like hope in face of direst traffic,
a greater growth than evil
in London's plastic life.

So good for you, I say,
and all others in the Flatlands of decay,

while Islington despairs and dies
grow acorns, grow flowers, grow old
tenderly tending your lives:
for the organic alone will fill space,
the acorn inhabit the abyss.

Tidying up

Ghosts of fog flee screaming
up the pounding Finchley Road
the sky is a no-sky, moonless
starless, empty, dyed
with a false spray-on light.

This pen tampers with lives
in the cold that racks
the vile felt of November air
in West Hampstead streets:
it presumes on the unutterably human.

It presumes on the unutterably human
loving that they love what they love
trusting that they are (really)
sensitive ghosts of a mutual reality
that will always need tidying up.

In Praise of Bus-stops

The evening sky is a sort of off-licorice black
with shadowy cloud pats floating towards
embers of a sunfire, sunset
and in this dying of a long day's light
the view of an important memory:

stood at a bus-stop on the Avenue
long ago, the wide apron of pavement
caked with a hard northern ice,
the wind blowing soft new flakes in the faces
of stupidly beaming shops.
Where was I going that fretful winter evening?
To see the old professor, of course, who lessoned me then.

But, in another sense, I was waiting for my future
to come lumbering and skidding up the ice-sharp hill
in the shape of a big red grunting bus full of
light and warmth and old men's fag smiles
whose conductor was king of small change and the bully
of schoolboys, a master of incomprehensible jokes,
who could stop the world by the press of a bell.

It was at bus-stops I learned how cold life can be.
But I learned also the wonder of waiting and watching
the stars battle it out in suburban heavens,
and heard the screaming choir of words in my head
from the lonely vantage of a dog-leaked lamppost,
my first of a million bus-stops.

In Praise of the Normal

(written after being the guests of two blind students)

They tell the time by a cuckoo clock's chime
Who like their own white faces will never see time.
She's big and madonna-pregnant, he's
A mind that sweeps like a March breeze
Down endless corridors of dark they must
Always inhabit. But at least they'll never see the dust!

In their narrow faintly fetid flat
Amazement not pity was the feeling that
Such a slow calm conformity
Could prevail in the face of disability!
Their books of braille, neat furniture
Two golden labradors of easy nature,

And mugs of coffee made for us all —
It was so very, very conventional
Though they would never see how normal
Who could only feel from wall to wall.

'London's not the place to bring up kids!' he said,
(Whose only fields and flowers are in his head)
'When I've my university degree
We'll be away into the country.'
In the dark hollows of his wife's eyes
A blind assent, a gentle unsurprize ...

It was all so normal like I say
To listen to them chatter in the usual way,
And never had I wanted so to praise
The normal in all my days.

Comfort beyond Comfort

Fine wine-flowered linen, brilliant cutlery
and waiters the slavish ghouls of gourmets:
in such a place I hit pure luxury,
a civet-scented life that never decays,
the old bitter snows and star-clotted nights
a memory to this fish-tank existence.
O the sweet polished girls with their tinkling gripes
and plastic escorts — how they breed resistance!
Then the music, this hurts, wallpaper sound
harmony itself marginalised, put on tap
like beer or God. Is anything now profound
in this democratic age of pop and pap?
With all the patience of an open book
a poet has to dream that there is hope.

On Not Looking Down on Anything

Born into the sound of bombs
that came out of life-thieving skies
in a little 'samey' avenue of suburbia
I was soon moved away
to a half-wild road lost in fields.
There I became a tribal child
among country shadows and lost songs
of birds, who clawed his way
to the top of trees, to a land of high branches
and imagination
where the world of the heart is.
And schooled in that rarefied atmosphere
of childhood, I have learned
never to look down on anything.

Outsider

(To the memory of John Tripp)

Because he thought things through
Because he stood up for truth
Because he then spoke out
And hinted at corrupted things
Because he was a democrat
In a democracy that was not
He found himself imprisoned
In polite gulags of the present
People are so good at building
For those who really care.

In Hampstead Cemetery

The souls are thinking in Hampstead cemetery:
'James Wilson, pasha, born Bridge of Weir 1842,
Died Hampstead 1908 — 30 years with the Egyptian Service',
I have a brief flash of 'Nilus' rolling stream',
See those silent sun-tortured sands,
Feel the vitality surging through decayed bazaars,
Recall the old joke about 'arabs' underpants' —
Egypt the essence of dirt, as here is proven
How, in any case, we all come to it:
'Earth thou bonny broukit bairn'
All around your ash-mouths yawn!

Monuments that age stretch down
Leaf-lined avenues of regret:
Today is grey as pathos and
The North London sky blank as any mystery.
I dwell upon life and death: an opposition that cannot be.
Mighty muscled workmen, many a sad whore,
The child delicate as a doily and prematurely dead,
The Big Wig and bourgeois nabob,
Sweaty char, anxious landlady, and those true lovers
Who knew the tender beauties of green and gold
Which alone flower in ardent hearts —
All these suffered cellular disintegration
(Wild-wombed women and hard men)
And were laid reverently or hastily
In the impartial, damp and dirty ground:
Some with small grey tongues of stone
To plead their last 'where'; others
Flattened under desperately-gesturing, angel-adorned
Tombstones that serve but to raise a laugh
Among the generations of a snickering future
Which also will pass in its shrill and frightened turn.

So what is this murderous death then?
Of whose kingdom on earth this cemetery seems
A brittle urbs, an endless downtown of doom.
I do not know, other than it seems
A very final change, a stroke of impotence
That renders null and void the white spurt of life.
Yet even as I walk these avenues of permanent autumn
Among mirthless stones of man's most desperate memories
Where blind carved angels mock us so,
I sense that unanalysable something of the living body
Still here: the souls are thinking in Hampstead Cemetery.

The Sensual and the Dead

A redbrick church, its door blandly wide,
A cassocked figure stood aside:
Sun, dead leaves, those who die —
        She looked at it, looked at me
In her death-struck eyes hungrily
The grey eroticism of endless life,
The love that makes a mistress or a wife.

A moment in the midst of living
At a street corner undertakers pushing
A pale-wood coffin on four wheels
(Even into brightest day night steals);
And she saw it, the silence in the noise,
Hesitated, almost lost her poise,
And looked from it to me
So that we both shared the mystery
That no matter how we soon pass on
Death must always make us one.

Cemetery in Salzburg

They lie within the mountains' hungry gloom
Family vaults like ancient cells of death
Behind padlocked ornamental gates
Bones and dust each in a private room.

Trakl's blue wind sifts the shrunken leaf
Gilded runes pit sable marble
With Hapsburg families and Austrian burghers,
The U.S. war dead lie in stark relief,

Confuse the present with their presence:
Some corner of a foreign field that is
Forever Yankee. A monument-mad place
That ends life's every licence

Without regard to national origin.
But it's still anomalous to find their names
Where the soul of Paracelsus broods,
Sun wears its sickly autumn grin

And clouds are white as knuckle bones
In Hitler's sky. Strange cemetery
Where strangers lie. It made me see
Death only lives in stones.

But life, the said-to-be transient,
Dances mocking, mocking-on
Like Paracelus who escaped the stake
Set free from death by words,
Which I think is what is meant.

A New Clarity

The Rue St. Germain
wallowing in traffic and sunlight
I drink my wine, smoke,
and think of Baudelaire
and the ever-creeping grey Seine.

To be here at last
after all the well-read years!
Yesterday at Notre Dame
A blind black beggar's eyes
forever whitened by the images' blast;

and Patricia weeping at
the stained glass glory of rose
'God entering in light
on Quasimodo Sunday'
such genuine moments of *éclat*

in the city of daylight dreams.
Words pumping endlessly
down wide avenues of thought:
from the Étoile to the Opéra
hope's long poem gleams.

Where people-watching's almost a duty
eating-out an art,
where paint-smeared skies recount
that words and life are one,
I melt into a new clarity.

The first Sunday after Easter is called Quasimodo Sunday

The Best of Life

I look upon the snow-cold blossom of blackthorn
And that golden ocean of wind-serrated corn
In the many seasons of past-perfect memory
That tell me the best of life is a dream, really.

The tired ponds of summer that are the newt's delight
Or the ice-crisp puddles that winter's children smite,
And thin veils of sun-teasing cloud that drift
Are the gentle deposits of a great scene that lift

Me into an old sanity beyond grief
Out of the sourness that makes life seem brief
And tells of the happiest part that's fixed
In this dear, darling world we have made so sick.

Epitaph for the Pastoral

Despair-moneyed days of pleasure
Of a youth long killed by lies
O to recall the sane grasses of once
When only alarmed larks plied
The blue-white drapes of sky!

Now under sweat-thumbed suns
Of wired-up and lacerated days
Is awareness only of blunted youth
—Chewing on plastic nothingness
In cars that graze the fields of time.

A Bright Imagined Home

Ah, how the dream bites! World is
And is not. Words of beauty like bluebells
In a May dawn's wood that we soon miss
For decay works even as goodness swells.
Poppies sleep as we sleep, but not the images
That rage on like blood in summer corn
Ambiguous creation that's nature-born
Never to die. Images live — O images!
Yet turn now from the dream, say that it's
Illusion, mere falsehood of the blood,
And what is left? A world of shoddy bits:
Life but a scrapyard of sparest parts
Where nothing, nothing, nothing comes to good
But ends in sorrow's breakage of junked hearts.
To survive the journey at all is going some!
But how, if not in dream's bright imagined home?

A Dark Pond like Truth

A dark pond coiled about by sweet green
and chuckling mud along its edges —
the lurk and thunder that is there! —
holding in still, dead rainwork wedges
of sun-filetted, unfettered clouds;
its deep distillation of memory's otherness
a standing glossary of images: crowds
upon crowds of waiting expression
that, like truth, has simply to be seen.

Therapy of the Sea

(South Devon)

In the thrall of the sea I have found
    my white unsettled self, often.
So often its innumerable tendernesses soften
    and its startling words
out of the yellow plastic beaks of gulls
    and the o-mouthed fishes
have settled the unease in my black blood.
    So I sing sea-therapy
under postcard-long skies of blue and fluff,
    and see my feelings settle
in little pools round the corners of squat rocks
    each prickled thought
dancing in translucence like fibre-glass
shrimps of dream that are no dream
    but real animalculae that haunt
    forests of weed and pulsing anemone.
Under all my suns of error and pain,
    evergreen sin and mistaken truth,
I can still call back the muse of sea,
    its love-lurch, its peace, its
frank pact of water and breath, its
    changeless morning of salt-starred sand, and
the moon of its night a silver spoon
    stirring the cupped waters of Torbay.

Some Irregularics for
Barbara Hepworth

In pumice stones of Cornwall
White holes of space.

In greeny parks
Worldwide
Rain slides your stone
And sunlight bites
Your lonely, lonely vision.

In oxydised bronze
And weird steel
All the grief at life's
Strange twists and turns
Of soul-shape.

How we gape in galleries
And gardens, heart-filled
And bone-chiselled
By your vision:
Everyway aware
Of your involuntary *suttee*
In that studio
By the brine-bright
Earth-bottled sea
The day the stones were pocked
With black holes again.

Scabbacombe in Winter

It is a cold and empty day
Nothingness of sky, nothingness of sea
Along the damp sand and shingle:
Looking down the cliffs into pale water
Mirrors is looking into me.

No one is here, no one there below
Where the rocks are broken biscuit,
No one. Only the sea's grey groan
And the strange roar of forever
In the non-existent wind.

I have to go down to that beach.
I have to now and again leave
The deceptive society of friends,
To talk with the trouble-laden sea
About the ends of ends of ends.

Over the singing shade and spongy
Patches of gladdening sand
To where sea swears in foam,
Curses; then intersperses vocables
Of sullen winter silver like a poet.

And as I reach the festering edge
Of marine life that is all life,
I hear busy Hampstead and all my
Deep world-love still in my head.
And I am both alive and dead.

The plain healing of winter sea
And the shiny pebbles pulsing:
The rooms of Hampstead in my head

Belong plainly in this pretty cove
Where I'm sea-driven into love.

How much is really all one, God
And the sea alone know. But
Coming to Scabbacombe Cove
In this dream of a poem
At the nearly seasonless time

Where clouds flake like sick white leaves
Off sky and gulls' morale is low,
I find the odd content prayer gives:
Where non-existence is strongest
Feel the life we live most lives.

Hampstead
22nd & 24th February 1990

Reading Nature

Autumn creeps in like a political statement
among tired people, where
once summer off-loaded ideas of sublimity
along sea-lagged coastal places.
But best somehow seems the day
when the rain of England falls
in a billion exclamation marks
on the dry skin of each grey-faced city.
Every phase of nature is a mood, a point of view ...
read its newspaper of weather
its reviews of flower-books, best-selling trees
and suburban scandals of grass and weed
that can never, never be repressed.
The green journalism that claims
someday the birds will outroar the cars,
and it will be Eden-time again. Someday.
Someday when someday will be now.

Ode on a Brixham Oil Drum

You still unsalvaged toxic drum
That leaking turns the loving tide to slime!
Where the wild gulls sadly cry and cough
Above the shining, perfumed petrol troughs
Of a sometimes inky-coloured sea
You loll, pollution's urn, among
The crispy bladderwrack and sea-anemone
And littoral's watery choking song
A tinny canister of greedy wealth
Where 'shell' means 'conch' and something else.
O 'memento vitae' and ravished bride
Of every calm and dirty tide
What a myth I see displayed
In the patterns on your rusty side!
What a world of suited satyrs
Fancy nymphs and money-makers
Is frozen there in stained relief
The immortal ugliness of social truth.
Yet, why lament this one old drum
Its rude and simple dented shape
When millions more are yet to come
To grease the world and make us gape
At the stunning dance of wealth and waste?
Why? Well, I guess, it is because
Where truth's no longer beauty now
Then all love's profit turns to loss
And on every oil drum's side we read
The same cold pastoral of greed.

Protosynthesis

All the sunlight catches me
    And it's in people also
A honey-yellow flood
    That turns to love I know,

As there's light in twisty grasses
    Turns to air's green fire —
And of watching that rough miracle
    Is something I'll never tire.

Hold still my window-eye
    Let love unknot the sight
Creep insect small and smaller still
    Into the things of light,

And back the stones will flutter
    Like their fellow leaves
So all may gather into mind
    Images in thoughtful sheaves.

Poem on My Birthday

Inching along the stone ledge
of a slippery century
and still wrestling with the same problem
how to praise
after Freud, Belsen, and the Bomb.

In a bind, a wedge
of bitter theory
I belay my syntax, each word a crampon,
and hold onto
a non-atheistical faith that is time-won,

not what taught to believe.
My breath smokes
in the cold air of too many deaths, I am
a body alone and tiring
but I still don't give a damn!

Getting on now towards
other folks'
fears, uncrossable precipice maybe,
the smart sun beams
out of the preposterous sky at me

and I lean my cheek
against the ice-wall
of reality and feel the throbbing in it
the frozen sperm
of infinity that has to be God-lit.

It cannot be quarrelled with

The little thing looks into your face
how shall you not break
that peaceful gaze of glass
that superb, that tiny space?

This child that one day will cease
to be a trusting animal, yet
still depend on you (despite
the ever-creeping slime of hate)

for every emotional solution.
How educate it and not
plough up (or down) arcadias,
their sheaves of windless trust?

Oh, honour the tender moments
on swings of every park,
set back a little while
your dark, and another's dark.

It cannot be quarrelled with
a flower, it is perfect
until the withering begins...

New World Order

The choice is you have
no choice but to believe
in the new white-edged world
that is coming to undeceive,

that would have everyone
consider a split-instant
their lurid little selves
not blubber, Can't, can't

but peel off the faded
graffitti'd transfers,
a wretchedly rational century's
cancelled posters.

Somehow, sometime back
smeared with ointment
of progressive hope we got
used to disappointment,

which is about as crazy
as endless economic growth
or technology's plethora of 'necessary'
needless products. Or both.

I would have you consider
smoking morning grass
or trees that belt the fine hills
or the minute mass

of the intricate blue fly
that troubles the nothing of air.
This because we are
in such images. All there,

though we feel only here.
Do unto ourselves as others
(things) do to us. Recognize
what we owe to others

(in whom we live
and have our being
as much as in the over-worked
demos of ego's seeing)

and we shall know ourselves.
The world is bread
and we are dough, the living
baked harvest of the dead.

A decent acceptance
of worldly things, everything,
means from scrappy sparrow to rheumy drunk
each is its own meaning.

Oh, be real now
do the action for its own sake
and for no devious cause. See
the white unravelling sea break

like rope on rock's teeth,
metaphor of wonder in every place
and there look upon your own
shining (tear joying?) face.

For the choice is you have
no choice but to believe
in the new white-edged world
that is coming to undeceive.

Having Her Back

Partitioned by a thin wall
from scandal of others' grisly lives
and all while birds are praising
their own domestic joys
is a sort of modern horror.

He loved her, she him, they
gave out in falsehood's insentient
social way. A pose? Who knows
anyone's darkly fibbing heart?
But, after all, that love seemed no more
than vapid chemistry of a fart,

as the quarrelsome descent
into dissension began
to poison paradise's neighbourhood.
Burdened like a thief she left
to gold-dig in distant parts;
while he turned thin and sour with hate
a blighted bachelor of spite.

Divorce followed and silence.
Thin white walls of houses became
once more partitions of thankfulness.
But a failed *sale* and more than
neighbours or solicitors knew
(time sometimes the evil healer?)
and she was back, a plague returned,
to trouble the village quiet —
the snakemeat still staining her lips
back with the fool she'd spurned!

Horses in Winter

Alone or in pairs like penitents they stand
in unholy wind at the bleakest edge
of fields of winter-gutted farmland
where inedible ivy clings to crazy walls
and trees offer bare ideas of form and age.
Some wear coats like men in shabby overalls
or chamois-naked stand log-still
fetlocked in a mash of ice and mud.
I marvel at their patience in such chill,
spare-ribbed statues of neglect whose
wincing flanks betray frost-detected blood,
and think they have a dream
of long-stalked days of green to come:
a special dream — they must! — that will preserve
a sanity and hope in horsey gloom,
which nature files for all who do deserve
some help through days of pre-death death
when wind would drill the stars from night
and freeze to glass bouquets a horse's breath
vainly cropping at rigid spikes of spite
and withered fodder far withdrawn
in nettled corners of each sunless dawn.

Remembering 'Workshop'

Does a whole decade like an iceberg lie
between the trivial now
and the razzamatazz of then?
That breathless antique upper room
of the 'Sixties over which presided
the ghost of Dryden
and the figure of Norman Hidden.
The beer and window boxes of The Lamb and Flag
the Muse in drag
and Eddie Linden his only poem
an epic in a carrier-bag,
with Madge Herron the authentic Crazy Jane
cursing the Bishops and keening for home,
and Ivor Cutler with cloak and stick
like a puritan misfit
turning the banal and verbally sick
into a newer species of worser wit.

In the room they came and went
talking of Marshall McLuhan
the air blue with the smoke,
the joke of a ham revolution:
with Adrian Mitchell shrieking 'napalm!'
and Norman still high on 'Spain'
when 'the poets exploded like bombs'
and Socialism was still a viable solution —
though anxious by then for the Party to be
if not clean at least calm.

O what it was to be young in that dawn
of liberty and the stifled yawn
to be in at the birth of hoped-for new writing
or at least present at Bohemia's last fling.
Time after time the words of the poets —

Pudney and Plomer, Patten and Spender,
all the famous were there —
crawled up the walls and fell in the beer
as poet after poet became a performer,
for to entertain was *de rigeur*
and quite the first principle of fashionable verse,
extending, in fact, the Carnaby Street curse.

Yet an era's slickest things,
its fashions, are soon over —
short the life-span of any false attitude —
and there is time for forgiveness.
As the Muse teaches (she who was rarely there):
greatness demands some gratitude.
So despite the bad verse and political nonsense,
the cheap dream of it all in its day,
it was a poetical experience
that Workshop gave in its way.

*'Workshop' was a monthly poets' discussion and reading
group, founded by the editor of the magazine New Poetry,
Norman Hidden, that held its meetings in the famous Dryden
Room over The Lamb & Flag public house in Covent Garden,
during the latter half of the 1960s.*

Spender at Torriano

Like a scene from Lautrec
that crowded, dingy room
in ill-lit Kentish Town:
the gleam of faces in sweat.

A figure of age-tarnished
elegance amidst rapt attention:
the creak of his lines and
the hovering, vanished

ghosts of the MacSpaundy club
and Barcelona's dead.
'Poetry's a côterie', he said.
'Aye, there's the rub!'

I thought; and thought of fashion
too. Then the questions followed
like ironic acid drops.
But where the rhythms of passion?

Gone into the black holes
of politics. All that was left
the immense generosity
of seventy cramped souls

glad of this one last chance
in a crowded dingy room
of ill-lit Kentish Town
to offer uncomplicated reverence.

John Clare, Scribbler

In my fireside corner, my retreat,
Safe from nothing but the winter's sleet,
Beneath sour thatch and sooty smell
In this cottage I write and inly dwell.
Time here is but a distant ache, a pain
Where I scribble myself slowly insane
In the unforgettable dream of a girl called Mary
Whom I somehow failed to marry,
And of the ever unnerving joy of flowers
That bruises my heart in silent showers.
Ever the twain must meet in me: the lover
First, then that world-embracing mother
Of every tiny or tremendous thing I see
From purple orchis burning silently
To lightning's co-ordinates that move
With Nature's frightening cry of love.
Unfaithed, and therefore without hope, I praise
Still my infant paradise of days
And watch myself die like Swordy Well
And scarcely ever feel other than unwell
Save when caught in words' pure flow
I re-envision that never fading glow
Of moments simple, tearless and profound
To which I am forever bound
And see within my inner summer corn
The comic landrail, and am glad that I was born.

A Critic in Brighton

(for Derek Stanford)

1. Station buffet

The yellow plastic of the place
like run butter, and you there
old-fashioned man-of-letters
in felt hat and tweedy suit
dreaming to urn hiss and clatter,
your mind as ever in
the kitchen of words not food.
My first sight of you, old chap,
for many writing years
but it is the same sharp face I see
and bright taut smile
playing on dry lips,
a small moustache of truth.
Old so-and-so of words
how easily you slide
into the pure poetry
of good conversation, yours
a wine spiced with nutmeg
rich in reminiscence
and vintage acuity.

2. Pavilion Gardens

Trees surround the parkly green
rubbing leaf and branch in August blow
that curls up trenchant streets
from the Channel down below.

Royal Pavilion's minarets
are stucco'd cardboard at the least

and every circling vehicle
a street-wise noisome beast.

The gazebo squeaks with music
deckchair bermudas sag or flap
as hundreds come to chatter
slump or eat or nap.

While three of us have travelled
half England's southern end
to ply you with tea and cakes
and question you, my friend,

because your words are dyed
like Tyrian cloth of time:
the very fibres of experience
of a mind that never was supine.

In gardens now at noisy noon
among Brighton folk and others too
this fond re-union occurs
that owes the most to you

who loves the life that passes
in and out of books and can recall
all the modern makers who
for the Muse's sake surrendered all:

yet not one of them you'll dub a fool
but allow every foible, fault or antic
confining your wit to works
as becomes an able critic.

And as you range among
the minnows, sharks and whales
in the sea of modern verse
we note your humour never fails.

For as each name was uttered
of magazine or man we felt
once more that power in words
that makes dull history melt:

a liberality of thought
and deep deliberation
of one who still believed
best poetry's celebration.

3. Cafe Tarde

In a cat-napping yard
where sun slept in geraniums,
boxed-in square of wood and stone
partially glass-roofed, alone
the three of us in a cafe took
a last half hour of you
before catching the train again
for the long haul home to Devon.

A touch of creamy froth on 'tache
from your coffee as we talked,
a last few perceptive thoughts
on the poems of Yours Truly:
the same calm understanding
unabashed by person or by place,
as you displayed so amply
that love of subject giving the feel
of what lies hidden in the least of words.
Seeing behind verse's secret shutters
the pure chemistry of sincerity,
that working of imagination through defects
which the honest critic detects
with as true a gift as any poet's.

Later, parting at the ticket barrier
you waved your stick and walked away
as much an anachronism today
as those who still find time to pray,
yet richer by far and happier
in this shared starlit prison
where I remain the poet
and you, dear friend, the critic.

Church Souvenirs

'The parochial authorities of St. Giles had the church repaired.
They took advantage of this circumstance to open the poet's tomb,
profane the leaden coffin, exhibit the bones for a shilling, and sell
them piecemeal.'

Emile Saillens: 'John Milton, Poet and Polemist.'

In the chancel moved slabs slide and bang,
Stone grinds on stone above the man
Whom Marvell would not let them hang,
Who *justified the ways of God to man,*
Told off Salmasius and Cromwell taught:
The poet who walked in mankind's first garden
And met God and Adam in Artillery Walk,
Fell victim after death to pagan Mammon.
For profit, sport, revenge, who knows what?
Parochial clerics of Cripplegate laid bare
John Milton's bones for all to leer at,
The fee one shilling, and later sold them there
For more than that to any passing ape—
Serving then, as now, those who only stand and gape.

Rupert Brooke on Paignton Sands

(for Dannie)

The souvenir shops are locked
in an out-of-season sleep
sea grinds slowly against
Paignton's gingerbread sands,
while fish-silver drizzle falls
rotting the pier's loose planks
and old people in nursing homes stare
into the beautiful nothingness of air.

In this unliterary place
where gulls slag off the sea
and seaweed hums in green piles
like Neptune's dung
Rupert Brooke once strolled, sepia'd
in a more certain age,
his brindled hair slicked
by the same driving rain
and left a sonnet a mile away
inscribed on the edge of the bay.

Osip Mandelshtam

It was for a freedom of...the image first
That he would roll the sun away
Submit to concentration camps of suffering,
Political barbed-wire surrounding.

Then for the right to write what he wanted:
The decadence of exploding flower bowls
And Georgian princesses with snowflaked lashes
And music in a great glass station.

So he made a lampoon on Stalin they say
And was transported neatly unsweetly away
To the heavy dull night of numbed Siberia
There to dream of a greater freedom and die.

A man for all freedoms perhaps?
No one's contemporary, no brother of now
He would reach back down the steps
Of the years like Senghor to the hands of his dead.

Not to be useful nor social but beautiful:
'So that the blue foxes in their primitive beauty
All night long may shine at me —
And a pine tree reach up to a star'.

This was the freedom that could not be crushed,
Never is, the immortalisation of moments
By which the hushed world really lives
And for which the idle, useless poet waits

To capture for you and me some truth
Something of that fire-of-forever, that breath
Which underburns the grey day world
And makes us want to worship and to weep.

For something like this did Mandelshtam die.

Poem written at Dannie Abse's desk

'Come on, fair do's', you will say,
When one poet asks another
To look after his desk
He is not expected to be other

Than a caretaker of cantos,
Securer of stanzas and stationery,
Riffler of the odd line or two
Some paper clips and free use of the glue.

But to write at your desk!
And not a letter or two
(His pen scratching your surface!)
But a poem (even two!):

Your Muse and him having it away
While you are away,
Laughing and giggling or seriously making
On your polished top.

It chokes you to think
Not of the risk of spilled ink
Or deplorable rings of careless coffee cups,
But of the barefaced cheek of it:

A poem (even two!) at your desk
Your altar of inspiration.
You gasp outright and ask:
'Oh, friend, how could you?'

Death and the Poets

Peter Porter, Dannie Abse
    and of poets many another
are more afraid of death than was my mother—
    and they are still alive!

But should they not try to see
    some good in the old rascal?
Why not be thankful for the inevitable
    end to life's bee-hive

of crazy competition and inanities?
    Were it not for leaden kisses
of the shifty hitman who never misses,
    the supra-vengeant sanction

poets curse even more than weather,
    the first tyrants would still rule
and each of us be slaves as well as fool.
    Because of death none can oppress forever.

Of course, death won't improve it's true,
    yet death deserves from poets
a better press than currently it gets.
    Some credit, as it were, where credit's due.

If only because, whatever we say,
    death and truth are closest friends
who never confuse means with ends;
    and because, well, someday
death always gets its own back anyway.

The Sexual Agony of Samuel Taylor Coleridge

I

The wind that left him breathless
was Beauty's wind —
it melted stars before his eyes
and brought down their meaning;
but the itch within his penis
for many an Abyssinian maid
made his philosopher's ordered thoughts tortured,
turned his art towards
orgasmic founts and fervid pleasure domes
and 'caverns measureless to man'
till his madness became our madness
and we, suspending disbelief, are glad
of the frank and dirty struggle
with the poor despised body
if only for the sake of such beauty —
its mother-of-pearl agony.

II

'And it was ever thus ...'
Coleridge not the first
will not be the last
to find the pure mind profaned
by life's ticklish trivialities.
Workers in fields of whatever green sublimity
aflame with sunlit song
will always find
mud on their boots sometimes;
nor can we pace city rooms in joy

without finding how much
flesh is tied to flesh.
But the wisdom such struggle teaches
is liberation, not from the body
but of the mind. And by donning
the mantle of the ageless sage,
like Coleridge, we find
out of the rage of disgust-filled passion
power to fashion vision:
even in the bowels of a rotting sea
discover such plagues of snakely beauty.
And, later still, on repentant land
shrived and cursed but never cured
we, too, perhaps may strew
life's path with golden forms
of Imagination's re-made world.

At the Grave of S.T.C.

Ah, supersoul, you plead for mercy
Now among the yellow hirsute angels
And pitchy little devils of eternity!
Do you know, S. T. C., a small child
Plays with a toy and yells and yells
Around your bluestone grave, wild
Where I stand in St. Michael's church?
A rude brat of modern innocence
Oblivious of time's tedious lurch
Even in this cold place of reverence.

At my side another poet stands.
One like you adept at astral physics
Who clenches his subtle body's hands
And cries tears of metaphysics:
Yet I know for all our intellect
His, yours and mine, time's traffic
Takes away that childlike gift
Of awful innocence which can lift
The veil and golden every gloom: terrific
In its simplicity. So, coming to your grave
In this church of embrowned pews and
Ghost-grey light, what best I'll save
In memory is the unholy sound and
Baby joy of a small irreverent boy —
His self at one with God's own will? —
Playing with a blue electric toy
Today on autumn-varnished Highgate Hill.

The Cancelling of Doubt

The day the glistening tempest
rolled by the summer woods
he first suspected gods —
it was like being lost yet not lost,
alone with the furies of that day.

He flung himself upon the ground
and watched the lightning spike the air
black as doubt upon the moor:
the impossible blue-bright light banged
truth out of fear and it seemed

a great vitality slithered by.
Wind wailed and rain skittered down
and there was something in being alone:
he heard the scattered birds sigh
and flayed insects cry where he lay

amidst stunned grass and futile shrubbery.
By the rocking world fascinated
it was as if he waited
not for the storm's going away
but for something no one could explain:

the answering flash of passion in the dark.
But soon he would grow older
and begin to wonder
at his perilous infancy
and doubt the very glory that was there.

Yet in any anxious midnight dream
flecked with inexplicable light
the shadows and the fright
of lost times would return again
and in memory doubt would cancel doubt.

Lucy and her Colonel

'From a literary point of view no biographical work of the time (the period of the English Civil War) equals in interest... The Memoirs of the Life of Colonel Hutchinson, Governor of Nottingham Castle and Town, etc. written by his widow Lucy...'
Cambridge History of English Literature

By candlelight in that cold castle
I had made warm for him, we talked
In the anxious nights and days
Before God and Oliver changed everything
At Marston Moor, and Royalists were
'As stubble to our swords'. Yes,
I think of all those times past since
First he came to dwell at Lincoln's Inn
And woo'd me for fourteen fair months
Beneath close oak and elm, among greenleaf
And roses by the trampled high of Holborn.
Was there ever such a courtship by a soldier,
A man of God, yet one who played so well
Upon a woman's love-taught heart?
He won me then in my wild-bird days
And I was ever after loyal to him:
As who would not be to a man
Whose strength was tempered by a holy heart?
Not in all the years that followed —
Such years of tempest and animosity
Cruellest for those of us directly destined
To tread the sickled road of politics
And bear a greater share in our own lives
Of the unwonted bloody brunt of civil war —

Was there ever blunting of resolve or peace for us.
Yet from the time my dear man governed
Nottingham Castle, that sanctuary so many found,
To the day they brought him dying home
From Sandown's darkest dungeons —
Where lack of care had quenched his greater flame —
Those, our candled evenings of closest talk,
Were very heaven and reward enough for any woman.
I who had had eight tutors as a child
And was for my time much overtrained
Was every bit his educated equal
And some might say his book superior;
Yet I had not quite the soul and passion
Of one who said: 'We are but servants
Of a God who would have a change wrought
In this land. No more a king omnipotent,
But upright men to hold the future's sceptre
And signal from this time forever
Individual freedom is the goal of power.
Love of man and love of God to be
The governing truth, as truth itself is all.'
By the single leafing of that frail light
To hold this man within my arms,
To pour a loving oil upon his flame
And supply his lack with my soul's plenty
Made me a very queen and for a short time
His equal sharer in that state of good sublime
Which is at the heart of every human love
For such as naked join together flesh and word.
And when he was gone, my regicide,
I wrote his life in the fair plain prose of truth
Rebutting calumny and told not every puritan
Was 'morose and melancholy and illiterate',
But many such as he were brave and thoughtful
Deeply wise and holy, as best men have ever been.

To Elizabeth

And this comely dame
She dwelt in Sothray
In a certain stede
Biside Lederhede...
And come whoso will
To Elinour on the hill,
With 'Fill the cup, fill!'
        from John Skelton's
        'The Tunning of Elinour Rumminge'.

Daughter, you are immortalised in Surrey.
To you and your husband I drink at the pub
where chickens shat in the vat at Elinour Rumminge's tunning.
And I think of that most realistic poem
in the English tongue (Chaucer notwithstanding)
its seedy and sawdusty scene set
in The Running Horse at Leatherhead,
where drabs and crones and easy-virtued wives,
good gossips and bad virgins cackled and droned
and were covered in lice and scabs,
poor needy and desperate females who gathered
for a nectarous pint of godless Elinour's brew —
a foul brew of Christ-knew-what that turned them each
to petticoated toss-pots who flew
round and round the room with banging dugs for wings
and up to some medieval bacchic heaven by the dozen.

But for no conduct the least like theirs
in genteelized Leatherhead now devoted to the Lady Hygeia,
a most unpopular deity in medieval Surrey,
Daughter, you are immortalised
(insofar as poetry can still perform its ancient function)
for choosing to reside within sneezing distance

56

(spitting now being forbidden) of that goodly
ancient ale house which foully earned
(or at any rate earned for its foulness)
several hundred lines of good hack laureate verse
and where the beer, if not as interesting, cannot be worse
than in its more famous talked-of tunning times.

In short, Daughter, you are praised for having led
your number-lisping dad to Leatherhead
and found for him, perched on a low knoll
beside the beery frothing River Mole,
a poetic local of the very first water.
                              Thank you, Daughter.

A Charm against Loss

I would just keep
the country for me
as an old apple
in the grubby pocket of the city,
and from time to time
take it out and see

it had not shrivelled
altogether but was
a still ripe reminder
of what I love because
in streets one needs not food
but charm against the loss

of mist-growth, roots
and sandy sun,
of long still waters
fields where horses run
and wind-mocked leaves
that whisper: Life is never done.

Ghosts

Once in a garden with Tudor-red walls
Stuffed with saxifrage, roses, hollyhocks and light
And some vine stems crawling on those walls
And slowly ripening plums at branches' height
I saw two revenants stood side by side.

The one a cavalier in plume-swept hat
Dressed in grey with pale blue sash and sword:
The rounder-headed other grimmer than that.
Both were still and never said a word,
Not battle-weary now nor visibly scarred.

And for a second I saw into their souls.
The cavalier self-willed of careless hubris
Had died at Naseby for King Charles
Whose command alone he set above his own, this
Well-bred, dauntless, dashing loser.

The other had fought at Cromwell's side
At Marston Moor but become Royalists' 'stubble',
Cut down despite a purer spiritual pride.
Strong men who had seen no end of trouble
All through sad impassioned lives

They stood before me ghosts of glass.
And in the green and roseate radiance of that garden
I knew what had come to pass
For them in death: both, both entirely human
Now as sucked away on flowers' breath
They faded into brickwork red as death.

The Peculiar Taste of Wild Olives

(i.m. Robert Graves)

Wild olives out of red earth
(Blood of past praise and death)
first tasted in a crooked orchard
that clung on crumbling terraces —
the peculiar taste of wild olives
all the green of the world
in their green smooth skins.

High above that valley
where the roofs of Soller swam
in incalculable light
it was a taste
bitter as Spain's history
yet simple as poetry.

All of our long climb
through the small sierras
we savoured it
the peculiar taste of wild olives.
It was like having tasted
civilisation
for the very first time.

A Beautiful Interruption

This morning shadowed by Regent Street's
Jaded architecture of enlightenment
The world blew up in a kind of glory,
A new faith:
Red buses and fat vans belched
And farted their blue cancer-mist
As they always do night and day
In that long curve of soiled elegance
That north-lit outlet of Piccadilly's crazy circus.
But, still, it was there, a window-leaking beauty
A smoochy miasma out of Soho
And the gilded Cafe Royal
With its stuck-up reminiscences
Of vanished literary life.
I saw it beneath the spinning-top of sky
From the clockwork heart of modernity's noisomeness,
And a carpenter saw it too, working
On a shop-front's broken blind,
Gave that same smile out of grime
Joseph gave to Jesus the occasion
Of an earlier ineffable interruption
To the headlong careering of the workaday world.

I should like someday...

I should like someday to lean
upon an old tree, the gleam
of sudden sun and passing cloud
a mixed and lavish light and shade
in its stubborn leaves (an oak
maybe or tired old elm?), and
enter once more that world of nature
that so long and so much passes by
those who in cities live and die.

Smell the ransom garlic rising
from among the grass-ringed roots,
hear the chaffinch slash the air
with its sharp, sweet-metal call,
touch the yellow stippled points upon
moss-green powdered bark
and feel that glassy dream,
that unity, that dripping stream
wash over me again,
and what no words can describe, descry:
a whole world in passing undecay.

Love on the Headland

Stood on a windy headland
We two, the blued sea grand

But summer-lazy as the small
Rock-lizard that sees all,

Moves like green lightning over stone.
We most remember when most alone.

Thrift shakes pink punk heads,
Bride bells of campion give way to reds,

Pin pricks of blood in golden moss.
Solitude, beauty at the heart of loss,

Into its vast space flood other faces:
Shapes whose warmth life graces.

The swaying cloth of tide below
A squeezed-out rhythm we know

As, sinking in the green calligraphy
Of grass, we make love's history

Again. And from the dream of mind
Withdrawing, see all by being blind.

Love on the Channel

Depth of what sea under this keel?
Rubbish of what hidden paradise?
The channel steamer rocks in vile swell.
All that matters is what we feel.

Raise eyes to the glister of star,
Her hand cool with a wanting love:
Nothing greater than that if it lasts.
Hold onto it in the beery sickness of a bar.

The sweet electric flesh disturbs, calms.
On the long swill of channel other boats.
Lights that dress in other silks soon fade
In the immortal murmur of her arms?

The Inspirer

Touching the water-colours of day
where clouds are like patterns on a window
I feel my way to visible themes

drift into intricacy of flower mouths
or turn a live moment to dust,
go longingly away on a clippered sea

become insect-eyed but tenderly precise
by pushing back varnished air
and breathing myself into stillness.

I am a painter now talking colours
a musician drawing forth notes
or a sculptor chipping marble thoughts.

But none of this is reaching enough
to get the visible joy out of waters,
those atoms of belief from a tree.

It's there, though, luminous after rain
purer than pain or innocent's idiot grin;
and the smooth shaper within

touches words into paint-sure place
turns out poems, songs, vision
making all real seeing a song of one.

Fenland Scene

(for G.P.)

Spasmodic spans of diluted sunlight
Arching a fenland reed river
Through small warnings of rain (on-faced
Filings of scrappy metallic clouds)
Cast into brief relief a rotten jetty
And a ruined inn, both dead
To usage and pleasure.
On the river's deceiving glass two ducks
Scribble their own quick comments
Which no light will ever make readable.
Only the greedy words of men ever aspire
To grasp and say what solution, what loss
Lie in every such abandoned scene.
And, also, what it may truly mean.

Is it so much, so great?

'*No worst, there is none*'
            G.M. Hopkins

Is it so much, so great?
We make much of the littleness
that is us, *us*.
Great generals! Great ghosts! Great griefs!
We tramp about the office carpets,
life's 'playing fields',
yell: '*here we go, here we go, here we go!*—'
Where? If not to the
Landscape-of-the-Very-Ugly-Ego?

Is it so much, so great?
Running about with our chests open
(and our mouths even wider)
showing our bleeding hearts
Lord, Lord haven't we suffered?
How we deserve, deserve
the Land of Milk and Honey,
that Welfare State of Spirit
with its love-and-money!

Is it so much, so great,
important
this pumped-up being
driving arrogant highways
under only one sun?
Not for a moment, dear thing,
dear human
unless you can praise and bless,
bless and praise greatly, always.

Is it so much, so great
to forget yourself

under the wonder of blindblack
infinite fields
accept a billion blue stars
pulsing with happiness, love
and so much brighter,
better than your own ... ?

Is it so much, so great?

An Admonition

> 'The roof, the floors, are gone
> Stolen your sea-green slates
> And smithy-work from Gort' —
> P. J. Kavanagh 'Yeats' Tower'

Oh, you Irish, the way
you let things go to wrack and ruin!
Why, why, why?
Is it that like you like to die
you like things to die too?
Thoor Ballylee, tower that pierced
the blue creative heavens,
a shut-up sullen ruin;
Coole park with its nine and fifty swans
gone, gone, gone!
Well, thank God for poetry's
mirrored skein of gold
that weaves all these lost things
into men's common memory,
                        and sings.

The Call of Ariel

In the bitter winter wood's hard silence
or steamy corner cafes where
lightning strikes more than once
I've felt the bubbling warm-cold shiver
induced by His words at Her behest —
a slip of a fellow in an antique vest.

When the cuckoo blows its hollow raspberry
in Spring, or navvies clatter-drill
on the tarmac of a city's skull,
or I hear the bully-hoot of a ferry
getting out of harbour — I also hear
another echo like a note of wistful cheer

or even mischief in the heart of fear.
I never actually see this prankster,
whose job it is to slack the note of order
just enough to admit the dancer
amidst the staid diurnal company we keep
in suburban intervals between sleep and sleep,

but rather feel his impish tingle in the air.
He teases the slouching beast in me
to song, pinching poor Caliban to terror,
and has to do with words and words' mystery
and that magic island of a poet's dreams
where what is, is other than it seems.

It's absurd, of course, to think of magician and familiar
where every poet's an accountant or teacher,
but to deny the truth is actually sillier:
even the wisest man needs a helper
for, perversely, we cannot have freedom,
nor love, nor write poetry entirely alone.

And that's where this cousin of Eros comes in:
sprite of the sublime distraction
whose precise purpose, now and then, is to win
you to that more serious attention
needed for better understanding of the dream
and its paler copy that's a poem.

The Ever-New Place

In the ever-new place of dreams
where weeds are golden
and roses really rose

the leering dwarfs
are taught to smile
and other monsters tamed.

In the ever-new place
where dead friends dwell
love ambient circulates

its air of hotel-peace
with long vistas of sky
and sea at the end of lawns.

There the grace of you is flesh
and marble hands and breasts
a princess of light,

and we talk over worlds and words
like the poems of God
in that ever-new place of dreams.

Venus Urania

'For even as humane fury maks the man,
Les than the man: so heavenly fury can
Make man pas man, and wander in holy mist
Upon the fyrie heaven to walk at list.'
                        (*L'Uranie*, Saluste du Bartes, 1574)

In the days of my young road when
Clouds stepped down the dripping hills
Towards the birds and children
I first met you, remotely, then.

Your flesh wild white roses
Your hands whiter than Athens' marble
Your light-cold glances that shook forth phrases
From me that I might sing unending praises

Of your wet streams of love and fire.
A temple grows and walks a woman
And I forever pray there:
Priest of contemplation and desire.

All truth was, is in your glance.
Still you make me feel simple things:
Stars that on the waters dance
Leaves that die at Autumn's entrance.

The mature and kindly sense of heaven
Lies beyond each passionate embrace:
Your cool rain on this heated kingdom
Falls, and Venus is my religion.

Venus is my religion now
Where past and future merge in one,

For goddess of painful joy it was you
Taught how love depends upon what we know.

And so I've come to gather up the world
Take all its works and turn them into words,
And in the heart where you lie curled
Our intercourse of verse is told.

Pieta of the Muse

I had searched for you through dream
my supportive creature,
by river and black industrial stream
wandered plain parks
with their pee'd on trees and litter louts —
the untidy skies of God above
signatured with clouds of love
and everywhere the dying factories crouched.

In the street of some anonymous town
at evening shopping time
on a fiery summer's day's decline
I saw you who were almost mine:
by the waters of impotent traffic lapped
amidst crowds of passing people
a shining sister with a marvellous figure
and a small boy in your arms.

And how I strained to catch your eye!
Looked upon your bewitching profile
ever pensive in the midst of change,
saw the half-familiar trace
of goddess in your face
whose every lineament was holy, strange.
Then woke in joyful anguish still.

Places We Are Scattered

The empty shore at Rhossili
its sawdust dunes and wind-moan
that long blown afternoon of light
far from the settled walks and talks
of Epping's golden springs
or damp-fugged days
spent in irksome shadows
of dying cotton mills...
We are born to be scattered
in fine rooms or dull
leaving some of ourselves sticking
like fingerprints on the woodwork of time
in an old North London flat,
a waxy boarding house in Lyme...
The glassy membrane of a window
overlooking Regent's Park
watching ourselves head for Baker Street
down an avenue of blossom,
the winding ringlets of a slow fountain
and ducks scissoring the lake —
the future for us a procession
of place, mysterious but sure...
Salzburg, walking in Trakl's shadow
his blue words twisting in my head
and Mozart's musical precocity
piped instead of pop in trinket shops;
and stone dwarfs in the Archbishop's park
their grotesque curiosity
at my talk of Dannie in Golders Green
and Russel! raging in Venice...
And but yesterday was in The Wheatsheaf
with old Hugo Manning;
in MacDiarmid's tatty garden
a thistle in Lanarkshire;

or walking 'some near olive terrace'
discussing myth with Graves
while sunlight peeled its lemonskin
in trembling shadows of leaves...
Love, love it is that scatters us
we are seeds that
bright birds flush from sun,
or water that wherever poured
somehow never drains away.
Every place belongs to us, we to it.
Small units of decay we are
belonging to an undecaying everywhere:
but memory sleeps in every place
and keeps us alive in our scattering...

Out of Into
or
Truth's Process

Water-drops drying in white sun
On any branch or rock
Are little buds of eternity
Always vanishing out of sight:
Out of rain or spume words come —
Of their brief form take stock
They are the eggs of certainty
Truth laid down by light.

Lines Written after watching Interviews with Three Artists on T.V.

L.S. Lowry

Magnified offerings of hoardings
against smoked-up skies
a loud and dirty busy street
of frankly tatty shops
and L.S. Lowry's great awakening
outside Pendleton Station*.
I knew that hell's ugly world
so well thirty years ago,
and my words fell into line
watching him brushing-up
a strange industrial beauty
of mills and work-belittled people.

Augustus John

Augustus John
who knew the poets and the faces
loved the gypsies
their wild ways of woods
and roadside camps,
a bohemian who denied bohemia
and said life was 'one long agony',
he poured nervous colour
into uncertain lines of character
twisting every visage
to some painful gaze of himself.

* *Because he missed a train Lowry went back home and decided to take up painting to pass the time.*

Henry Moore

A giant of space
who made stone and bronze
and wood appeal.
With convoluting shape
and smooth unmeaning limb
he longed to relate
bodies to bodies
and weld the crying emptiness
of a faithless world
to the great silent plenum
that frightens every modern
Pascal. An artist not of beauty
but of truth.

Coda

Lowry building ex-nihilo
with each wet brushstroke,
John the passionate copyist
of all experience which lies in faces
like pools of stagnating water,
and Henry Moore shaping
out of ballooning space
with classic desperation...
three men made honest
by a common struggle.

Ambulances

A panic of blood and bandages
the white ambulance elbows its way
through surprised and half-indignant traffic
and we who are well feel safe today.

Death's drama is at the edge of everything
and serious men in sombre mood pretend to cope:
hearses are the sleek birds of endless night
ambulances the shrill doves of hope.

Streets, O the streets overflow with maggoty life
and love is poured from hearts in bucketfulls!
Money changes hands and pleasure smiles
but life is only lived because it lulls?

Every time I see an ambulance go by
I think of drama incubating in all of us
and how we must face up someday to terror,
know or not know what it is undoes

image from image, soul from body, love from love.
Do the cells go out the window really, and why?
Can the only point of living be to die?
Or is the world itself the neatest lie

down to its blackest fact? I cannot say.
But every time an ambulance goes by
and cars hold their breath and stare like cats,
it is a moment when I see men's fear is holy
before life's death-guaranteed mystery.

The Urbanised Soul

Always hesitating between here and there
Forced to stop at kerbs of shabby nothing
Valleys of infinite litter, alternately
Bitter and goldenly placid,
Strings of streetlamps that glitter
Needle a city's throbbing throat
(So vulnerable that jugular girder!)
Another 'she', mirror-image of whore,
Mother, troll of the concrete woods,
Or who knows who or what may be?

Soul in her glad rags or weeds of night
Treading on Coke tins and glass
When the drunks snarl by effing and blinding
Down the greasy streets of time
(Rain swills out their speckled vomit).

Standing back in shadows of green thought,
My thoughts touch her palpitating core.
Old and tender cow she is
A lady underneath, and
Knowing this I choke in the blind
Trickle of her silent tears,
Her horrid knowledge:

Nowhere but in dreams now
The saffron wheat, the untold paradise.

To the Humble Reader

You, reader, perhaps soured into sorrow
Or just scared, may come upon this page
In some second-hand shop of autumnal
Books. Perhaps you borrow

From a small North London library
Or in the sedater shires — who knows?
Well, this poem also is of one
Who has known grave unease of city

The coldly impersonal and captive light
Of shop-fronts and lamps that bathe
Such haunted faces: the many
Selves of us we hate and spite.

The broken pavements of the urbs
Like shards of flattened skulls,
None but oil-bespattered angels
Now seen: hell's images that disturb

Till you see, and I see, the anti-hope
Of the far too far-off stars
(Irrelevant now it would seem)
Scattered down the random slope

Of an unloving and awesome universe.
This coreless world an old brown apple
And we on it longing for
Yet fearing death — or worse!

It is the peacelessness of the whole
Set-up we cannot abide:
Empty suburbs where only violence
Is going on: it takes its toll

Of all those finer feelings which
One geranium or forget-me-not
Can summon: a flaring gift
To make the white day speechless, rich.

You, reader, perhaps soured into sorrow
Or just scared, I am with you —
By secret fires and new beginnings
Is the shape of our tomorrow:

We are small, but we can wait...

Standing on the Brink of Light

Shards of the age
Half-finished monuments
By giant sculptors
The Dartmoor tors
Polished by sun's monocle-glint
Become shapes of fantasy
Points of reference
When shadow curtains
Draw slowly aside
To reveal green valleys
And purple-speckled plains.

Let one hand press rockflesh's
Immovability
The other finger dream of light
And, if you can do it,
In a moment of self-absence
Of deep concentration
Rock will turn back
To intricate fibres of old existence
And light transform
To pure points of meaning
Awaiting the surprise
Of the still persistent word.

The Witness

When something of me outleaps with a bird
Above the crowded creaking wind-fingered wood
Or when overlapping clouds have stirred
Imagination to admit a somehow greater good
Than the mean temporality of a too-glum city
Then, and only then, in feeling more than human
Do I laugh and think myself into being human.

Is being human knowing what I really am?
Or forgetting all I ever did or did not do?
No, it's when I hear the sea's ecstatic slam
And sense a silence after violence coming through
Like an unspoken echo to every thought of *me*
Then I know that time has given way to stillness
And what I am is — O universe — your witness!

Of the fly that sucks the bleeding plum, raindrops
Slithering windowpanes, morning mist upon the moors
Like puffs of gunsmoke, or the seedhead that wildly pops
Disclosing mystery's many outstrewn doors
Which we call flowers — fragile stars of certainty
Whose beauty signatures our littleness of days
And guarantees our own creative blaze

That stops each passing moment of oblivious time
With these words: *World, I do not understand you*
But somehow know that you are mine —
From sun-satisfied fields fed with dew
To snow-capped mountains far more mighty
Than all save bitter sea and barking ocean —
Mine, in a loving mirror of stilled emotion.

My White House

My white house
to which the blue sky sticks
home is there
the garden of many summers
and dull winters
by the quiet folding of sea.

There where flames
valerian, the leaning foxgloves
and toadflax
in tangible, esurient,
time-scaled walls where
dragon-memory slumbers

in a Devon garden
without history whose sun
and salt-breathing wind
make myth and beauty —
the quiet anonymous years of a
garden's poetry.

The Still Place

The still place that stands gleaming
in spring's generous morning sun,
shawled around by distant traffic hum,
is a light-bespattered piece of peace
a colour-woven space of sight:
a lawn pierced by rugged trees
barked like pitted rock suggesting
sculptured, twisted, wilder places
with fingered lozenges of leaves
that twitch in a breeze of green thoughts,
while on the ground and all around
are spurted clumps of white and blue flowers.

A small in-city choice of nature's captured space,
glory of immediacy in scintillating ordinariness
stunningly speckled with unbroken meaning
like a friend who never fails to show up
with some exciting snippet of human news,
or ring-doves pecking at bluebell seeds

On the Craving for Silence

This multi-structured mind
I find myself in
has shadows, streams and windows
and that on-one-level-sun
that syrups walls and sills
and makes every day
a pale cliché of the last.
But I cannot write:
Only a little Fountain lent
                    Some use for Eares,
now thought is deadened so by noise
of fast jet fart and brazen 'pop',
and every natural note of joy
or suffering cry
is overlaid and turned to phonic slop.
All I can do is concentrate
on subtle tones of memory
and immerse within
this bookish sea
whose turning waves of words
respond to rhythms
of moons and stars
we never know or see
or need to hear.

MOTET: The Conventional Man

I love the wristy ping of a digital watch
and every kind of pasty clock,
I love the way the stair-rod rain
thrashes safely the window-pane
for I am your habit man who loves to be
the soul of regularity.

In gardens of green handkerchiefs
between bungalows and semi's
are the flowers of Saturday and Sunday
and these I count the back-up hobby
of a life that depends on means not ends
and such user-friendly friends.

I have my problems, though - don't we all?
a son who is as sullen as a crow
a daughter who rooms in chaos
but you may be sure I successfully interface
with such reality by means of my usual
meticulous attention to detail.

The world is my desk and all things on it
must be kept in order. In the
New Beginning was the Number not the Word.
And in my insured beginning I heard
One number-crunching voice utter
Get a computer!

Since when, with everything at last screened
my sense of duty has born fruit
I live on Apples and Apricots in a bleeping paradise,
where I have the power, the data and the choice:
which is to say, the means to make for all
a world that is perfectly normal.

MOTET: The Irreverent Man

Safety, safety, this even the poets cry.
Don't rock the boat or else you'll die, die
into the black hole of the Public Eye.
But what does he care, or what do I?

Smoke, eat, drink, most of all think
and share the vagabond stink
and listen to that tell-tale clink
of truth not money. Yes, *think!*

Spare me the good-bad causes and
the bland lies of a bloodless land,
spare me the soft soap of the grand
their liberal principles like rubber bands.

Spare me the Media, spare me the Age,
spare me the educational cage,
spare me the groups out to 'encourage',
spare me politicians and their pious rage.

For I can only see the threadbare pose
of an emperor with no clothes
and the oddness of a poetry that thinks it's prose
producing beauties like the petal-less rose.

I swim in seas mountainous with self-pity
and wander streets of an alien city
whose days are philistine, whose nights are deadly,
but like the oyster try to be gritty

and now and then think the original thought
pearl of no price that cannot be bought
believing in love whatever I'm taught,
and upsetting the consensus my chiefest sport.

So spare me, spare me anything you like
but not the hope that together we might
someday meet for a sensible talk
just how the hell you can always be right?

Love Motet

'Whatever we say is said against death'
Michael Hulse

Every love is unique. Am I unusual in saying this?
        It made the winter roads
        bright with kisses,
and summer hayhot and honey,
            passionate in the drooping leaves.

Even if the seas leap with delight at what you *feel*
        as death's quickly rusting guest
        don't invest the love machine
with more than working parts and arts
        of a heart everyone *has.*

Sticky with sunlight I leave golden fingerprints
            on her chalice and she smiles for me.
        I am recognizable by touch
        and she by a touching faith.
Like you say, there's no perpetuity in
        machines. Only in life in love.

Death is the ultimate proof and death has dominion -
        a spasmodic accident
        the race endures,
but not that we cover graves with stone
        the certain, solid thing.

I looked into living blue, her eyes, that
            long ago moment of light
        and I saw the stones crumble.
        O adversary of my life
we feed on different doubts, despair of such
        different beauties!

Language's Tool

Up North people always speak their mind
But is it a mind worth speaking?
Down South people rarely speak their mind
But is it a mind worth keeping?
A puzzle? No, just language's tool
Used differently, by the same simple fool.

EPIGRAMS

The Teacher

The teacher who considers the world his class,
The world considers a pompous ass.

A Born-Again Christian

He had to be a Born-Again Christian because
First time round he was such a dead loss.

Goodwill

If we two are destined in Heaven to dwell
Then better for me a ticket to Hell.

Youth and Age

What is youth?
Lies, deception and credulity.

What is age?
Lies, deception and incredulity.

The Last Sinner

In an age of sex and porn and every kind of filth
And unholy holy worship of the niceties of wealth
And getting what you can when you can
Because the rights of money have superseded those of man,
To the newest kind of puritan and moralistic joker
The only sort of sinner is a smoker.